Animal Homes

Birds and Their Nests

mourning warblers

by Linda Tagliaferro

Consulting Editor: Gail Saunders-Smith, Ph.D.

Consultant: David M. Bird, Ph.D.
Avian Science and Conservation Centre
McGill University
St. Anne de Bellevue, Quebec, Canada

Capstone
press

Mankato, Minnesota

Pebble Plus is published by Capstone Press,
151 Good Counsel Drive, P.O. Box 669, Mankato, Minnesota 56002.
www.capstonepub.com

062010
005856R

Books published by Capstone Press are manufactured with paper
containing at least 10 percent post-consumer waste.

Library of Congress Cataloging-in-Publication Data
Tagliaferro, Linda.
   Birds and their nests / by Linda Tagliaferro.
   p. cm.—(Pebble Plus, animal homes)
   Summary: Simple text and photographs describe birds and the nests in which they live.
   Includes bibliographical references (p. 23) and index.
   ISBN-13: 978-0-7368-2383-8 (hardcover)
   ISBN-10: 0-7368-2383-2 (hardcover)
   ISBN-13: 978-0-7368-5123-7 (softcover pbk.)
   ISBN-10: 0-7368-5123-2 (softcover pbk.)
   1. Birds—Nests—Juvenile literature. [1. Birds—Nests. 2. Birds—Habits and behavior.]
   I. Title. II. Series.
QL675.T325 2004
598—dc22   2003013424

Editorial Credits
Martha E. H. Rustad, editor; Linda Clavel, series designer; Deirdre Barton and Wanda Winch,
   photo researchers; Karen Risch, product planning editor

Photo Credits
Bruce Coleman Inc./Kevin Byron, 16–17; Roger Wilmshurst, 4–5
Corel, 1
McDonald Wildlife Photography/Joe McDonald, 7
Minden Pictures/Konrad Wothe, 21
Tom and Pat Leeson, 9, 10–11, 13, 14–15, 19
Tom Stack and Associates/John Gerlach, cover

Note to Parents and Teachers

The Animal Homes series supports national science standards related to life science. This
book describes and illustrates birds and their nests. The images support early readers in
understanding the text. The repetition of words and phrases helps early readers learn
new words. This book also introduces early readers to subject-specific vocabulary words,
which are defined in the Glossary. Early readers may need assistance to read some words
and to use the Table of Contents, Glossary, Read More, Internet Sites, and Index/Word
List sections of the book.

Word Count: 175
Early-Intervention Level: 16

Table of Contents

Building Nests 4

Eggs and Chicks 12

Keeping Nests Safe 16

A Good Home 20

Glossary 22

Read More 23

Internet Sites 23

Index/Word List 24

Building Nests

Birds build nests in trees and on buildings. They also build nests in cliffs and on the ground. Birds use nests to hold eggs and chicks.

finch with chicks ➤

Birds build nests with grass and twigs. Birds sometimes use mud to hold the grass and twigs together.

black-headed weaver ➤

Birds make holes for nests in trees, cliffs, or the ground. They dig with their bills or their feet. Birds may line their nests with grass.

pileated woodpecker ➤

9

Some birds build nests in one day. Other birds take two weeks. Eagles may take two months to build their nests.

bald eagle ➤

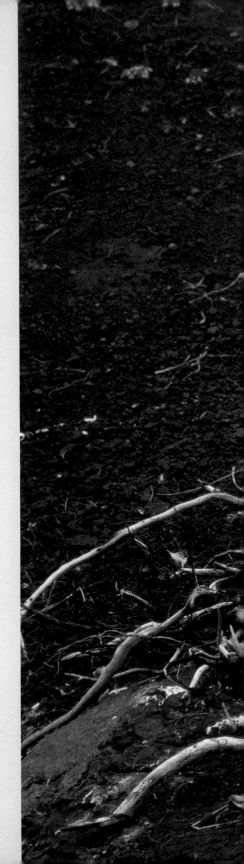

Eggs and Chicks

Birds lay eggs in nests.
Some birds lay just one egg
in a nest. Other birds lay
up to 16 eggs.

ruffed grouse nest ➤

Birds sit on their nests to keep the eggs warm. Chicks hatch from the eggs. Some chicks stay in the nest.

common loon ➤

Keeping Nests Safe

Birds hide their nests.

Hungry animals cannot find

the eggs or chicks.

American robin nest ➡

Trees and cliffs help protect
nests from rain. The nests
stay dry.

green-tailed towhee ➡

A Good Home

Different kinds of birds
build different kinds of nests.
Nests help keep eggs and
chicks safe and warm.

penduline tit ➤

Glossary

bill—the hard, pointed part of a bird's mouth; birds use their bills to eat, feed their young, carry twigs, and build nests.

chick—a young bird

cliff—a high, steep wall of rock or earth

egg—a rounded object with a covering or shell in which young animals develop; female birds lay eggs.

protect—to keep safe from harm

twig—a small stick

Read More

Frost, Helen. *Bird Nests.* Birds. Mankato, Minn.: Pebble Books, 1999.

Pascoe, Elaine. *Birds Build Nests.* How and Why. Milwaukee: Gareth Stevens, 2002.

Tagliaferro, Linda. *Robins and Their Chicks.* Pebble Plus: Animal Offspring. Mankato, Minn.: Capstone Press, 2004.

Internet Sites

FactHound offers a safe, fun way to find Internet sites related to this book. All of the sites on FactHound have been researched by our staff.

Here's how:

1. Visit *www.facthound.com*

2. Type in this special code **0736823832** for age-appropriate sites. Or enter a search word related to this book for a more general search.

3. Click on the **Fetch It** button.

FactHound will fetch the best sites for you!

Index/Word List

animals, 16

bills, 8

build, 4, 6, 10, 20

buildings, 4

chicks, 4, 14, 16, 20

cliffs, 4, 8, 18

dig, 8

dry, 18

eagles, 10

egg, 4, 12, 14, 16, 20

feet, 8

grass, 6, 8

ground, 4, 8

hatch, 14

hide, 16

holes, 8

mud, 6

protect, 18

rain, 18

safe, 20

sit, 14

trees, 4, 8, 18

twigs, 6

warm, 14, 20